REFASHIONED HARDWARE

FUN & EASY FASHION PROJECTS

ALEX KUSKOWSKI

Checkerboard Library

An Imprint of Abdo Publishing
abdopublishing.com

abdopublishing.com

Published by Abdo Publishing, a division of ABDO, PO Box 398166, Minneapolis, Minnesota 55439. Copyright © 2016 by Abdo Consulting Group, Inc. International copyrights reserved in all countries. No part of this book may be reproduced in any form without written permission from the publisher. Checkerboard Library™ is a trademark and logo of Abdo Publishing.

Printed in the United States of America, North Mankato, Minnesota

062015
092015

Design and Production: Jen Schoeller, Mighty Media, Inc.
Series Editor: Liz Salzmann
Photo Credits: Jen Schoeller, Shutterstock

The following manufacturers/names appearing in this book are trademarks: Crafter's Pick™, Craft Smart®, Krylon®, Liquid Nails®

Library of Congress Cataloging-in-Publication Data

Kuskowski, Alex, author.
Cool refashioned hardware : fun & easy fashion projects / Alex Kuskowski.
    pages cm. -- (Cool refashion)
Audience: Grades 4 to 6.
Includes index.
ISBN 978-1-62403-700-9

1. Dress accessories--Juvenile literature. 2. Handicraft for girls--Juvenile literature. 3. Jewelry making--Juvenile literature. 4. Handicraft--Juvenile literature. I. Title.

TT649.8.K87 2016
646.4'8--dc23

                    2014045318

To Adult Helpers

This is your chance to assist a new crafter! As children learn to craft, they develop new skills, gain confidence, and make cool things. These activities are designed to help children learn how to make their own craft projects. They may need more assistance for some activities than others. Be there to offer guidance when they need it. Encourage them to do as much as they can on their own. Be a cheerleader for their creativity.

Before getting started, remember to lay down ground rules for using tools and supplies and for cleaning up. There should always be adult supervision when using a sharp tool.

Table of Contents

RESTART YOUR WARDROBE

Hardware **TO** Fashion Wear

Get started refashioning! Refashioning is all about reusing things you already have. You can turn them into new things that you'll love.

Spruce up your **wardrobe** with hardware. Create fashionable shirts, belts, and bracelets. You can reuse things you have around the house. Or get supplies at a hardware store.

Permission & Safety

- Always get **permission** before making crafts at home.

- Ask whether you can use the tools and materials needed.

- Ask for help if you need it.

- Be careful with sharp and hot objects such as knives and irons.

Be Prepared

- Read the entire activity before you begin.

- Make sure you have everything you need to do the project.

- Follow directions carefully.

- Clean up after you are finished.

Basic terms and step-by-step instructions will make redoing your closet a breeze. These projects will help you turn hardware into one-of-a-kind fashion pieces.

HEAVY METAL FUN

You don't have to hunt through your closet to find cool stuff to remake. Look in your **garage** or basement. Or go to a hardware store.

Look for metal fasteners. Many small metal parts can be attached to clothes, jewelry, and even shoes!

HARDWARE TO REFASHION WITH

NUTS

STUDS

COTTER PINS

HINGES

BOLTS

WASHERS

BRACKETS

Refashion Ideas for Hardware

STICK TO IT

- Glue hardware pieces to a shirt with fabric glue.

- Use heavy-duty glue to add hardware to a purse or shoes.

TOUGH JEWELRY

- String nuts and washers onto ribbon to make a bracelet.

- Put keys on a metal chain to make a rockin' necklace.

TIE IT UP

- Knot ropes together to make a cool belt or a strap for a bag.

- Glue rope to a shirt to make a fashion **statement**.

7

TOOLS & MATERIALS

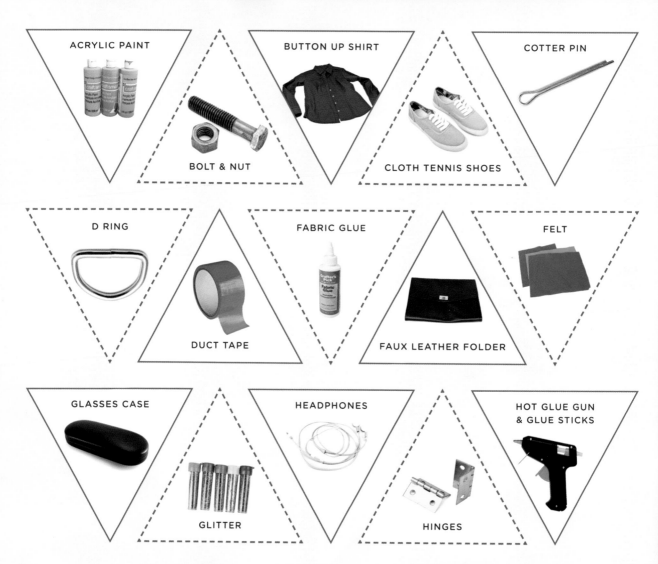

ACRYLIC PAINT

BOLT & NUT

BUTTON UP SHIRT

CLOTH TENNIS SHOES

COTTER PIN

D RING

DUCT TAPE

FABRIC GLUE

FAUX LEATHER FOLDER

FELT

GLASSES CASE

GLITTER

HEADPHONES

HINGES

HOT GLUE GUN & GLUE STICKS

HERE ARE SOME OF THE THINGS YOU'LL NEED FOR THE PROJECTS IN THIS BOOK.

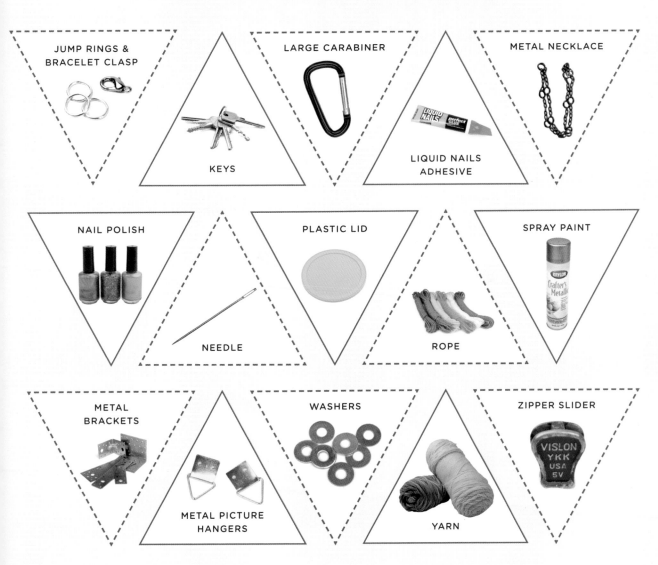

JUMP RINGS & BRACELET CLASP

KEYS

LARGE CARABINER

LIQUID NAILS ADHESIVE

METAL NECKLACE

NAIL POLISH

NEEDLE

PLASTIC LID

ROPE

SPRAY PAINT

METAL BRACKETS

METAL PICTURE HANGERS

WASHERS

YARN

ZIPPER SLIDER

STUDDED
GLASSES CASE

Get a Chic Clutch Purse!

1 Cover your work surface with newspaper. Decide how many washers you want to put on the glasses case. Paint one side of each washer with nail polish. Let it dry.

2 Glue the zipper slider to the front of the glasses case. Center it above the opening.

3 Glue the washers to the top of the case. Let it dry.

4 Put glue around the washers. Sprinkle beads on top of the glue. Let it dry.

Even Cooler!

Paint the glasses case first to add even more color!

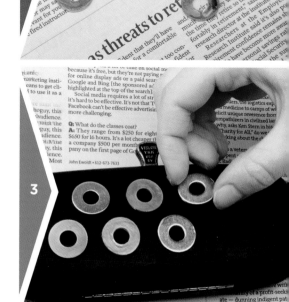

11

TUNED-IN
HEADPHONES

Listen to Your Music in Style!

WHAT YOU NEED

HEADPHONES
DUCT TAPE, 3 COLORS
RULER
SCISSORS

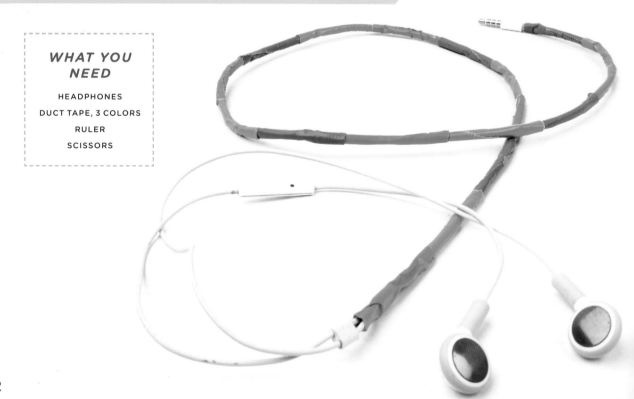

1. Lay the headphones out flat. Cut a piece of duct tape 1 inch (2.5 cm) long.

2. Wrap the duct tape around the cord near the plug. Make sure it is smooth.

3. Choose another color of duct tape. Cut a piece 1 inch (2.5 cm) long. Wrap the duct tape around the cord. **Overlap** the first piece ¼ inch (.5 cm).

4. Keep wrapping pieces of duct tape around the cord. Alternate colors. Cover the entire cord.

Even Cooler!

Add more colors to the mix for some crazy jammin' headphones!

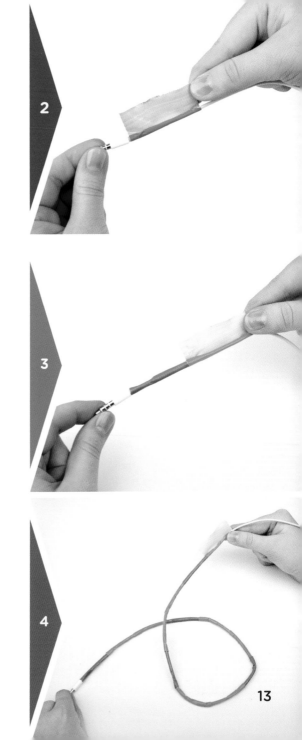

13

BRING ON THE BLING

Make Some Cute Kicks!

WHAT YOU NEED

PLASTIC LID
LIQUID NAILS ADHESIVE
TOOTHPICKS
2 METAL PICTURE HANGERS
CLOTH TENNIS SHOES
130 BRASS HEX NUTS

1. Put some adhesive on the plastic lid. Dip a toothpick in it.

2. Spread the adhesive on the flat part of a hanger.

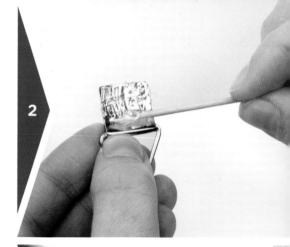

3. Press the hanger to the heel of a shoe. Hold it for thirty seconds.

4. Use a toothpick to put adhesive on a nut. Press the nut to the heel of the shoe. Hold it for 30 seconds. Add more nuts until the heel is covered.

5. Add a line of nuts along the front **stitching**. Let the adhesive dry.

6. Repeat steps 2 through 5 with the other shoe.

Even Cooler!

Paint the shoes with fabric paint before adding the hardware!

15

RAY OF SUNSHINE
NeckLACE

Let Your Inner Self Shine!

1 Cover your work surface with newspaper. Lay the cotter pins on the newspaper.

2 Spray the cotter pins with the spray paint. Follow the directions on the can. Let them dry for 6 hours.

3 Turn the pins over. Spray paint the other side of the pins. Let them dry for 24 hours.

4 Arrange the pins with the longest in the middle and the shorter pins on the sides. Put beads in between the pins.

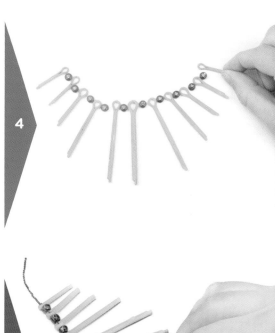

5 Use the pliers to remove the jump ring from the necklace. String the pins and beads onto the necklace in the arranged order.

6 Put a new jump ring on the end of the necklace. Close the ring with the pliers.

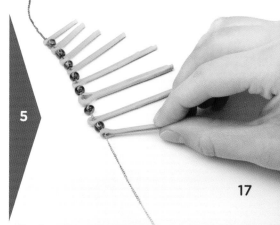

HEXAGON
BRACELET

Brace Yourself to Look Fabulous!

WHAT YOU NEED

NEWSPAPER

18 HEX NUTS

ACRYLIC PAINT

PAINTBRUSH

YARN

MEASURING TAPE

SCISSORS

TAPE

BRACELET CLASP

CRAFT GLUE

1. Cover your work surface with newspaper. Lay the hex nuts on it. Paint the nuts. Let them dry. Paint the other side. Let them dry.

2. Cut six strands of yarn 20 inches (50 cm) long. Tie the strands together 2 inches (5 cm) from one end. Tape the knotted end to a flat surface.

3. Separate the yarn into three sections of two strands. Braid the yarn for 2 inches (5 cm). Put a nut on the left strands. Push it up to the braid. Cross the left strands to the center.

4. Thread a nut onto right strands. Push it up to the braid. Cross the right strands to the center.

5. Continue adding nuts as you braid. Alternate sides. Keep braiding after all of the nuts are used. Tie the yarn in a knot 2 inches (5 cm) from the end.

6. Cut four of the strands close to the knot. Put the bracelet clasp on one of the remaining strands. Tie the remaining strands together. Dot the knot with glue. Cut off the extra yarn.

7. Cut four of the strands on the other end close to the knot. Tie the remaining two strands together into a small loop.

19

BRAiDED
BELT

Climb into Fun Fashion!

WHAT YOU NEED

ROPE
MEASURING TAPE
SCISSORS
2 D RINGS
HOT GLUE GUN &
GLUE STICKS
LARGE CARABINER

1 Cut three pieces of rope 71 inches (180 cm) long. Put one end of the ropes through a D ring. Fold the ropes over the straight side. Pull until all ends are even.

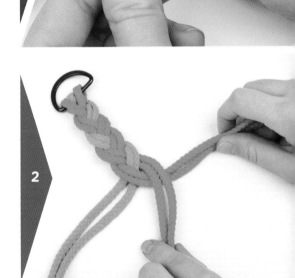

2 Separate the ropes into three groups of two. Braid the ropes.

3 Put the end of the braided rope through the second D ring. Fold the rope on top of itself. Hot glue the end of the rope in place. Let the glue dry.

4 Clip the D rings to the carabiner.

Even Cooler!

Add more pieces of rope for a wider belt!

21

CUTE KEY HATS

Unlock Your Craftiness!

1. Cut a 2-inch (5 cm) square of felt. Fold the felt over the top of the key.

2. Trim the sides ¼ inch (.5 cm) away from the key.

3. Remove the key from the felt. Punch a hole in the felt near the folded edge. Stick the key back inside.

4. Thread the needle with embroidery floss. Tie a knot at one end of the floss.

5. Push the needle through both layers of felt near a corner. Sew along the sides of the key.

Even Cooler!

Label your key hats with a Sharpie. Then you'll know what locks they open!

GeARED-UP
SHIRT

Get the Military Look for Less!

1 Cover your work surface with newspaper. Put the metal items on the newspaper. Paint the metal items. Follow the directions on the paint can. Let them dry at least 6 hours.

2 Cut a sheet of cardboard the length and width of the shirt. Lay the shirt out flat. Put the cardboard inside the shirt.

3 Arrange the metal items near the shoulders on both sides.

4 Glue the pieces in place. Let the glue dry.

Even Cooler!

*Paint **designs** on the hardware with bright colors after spray painting!*

UNHINGED
BRACeLEt

Get Your Wrists Glittering!

WHAT YOU NEED

NEWSPAPER

4 SMALL HINGES

NAIL POLISH

GLITTER

RIBBON

RULER

SCISSORS

26

1. Cover your work surface with newspaper. Put two dots of nail polish on each hinge.

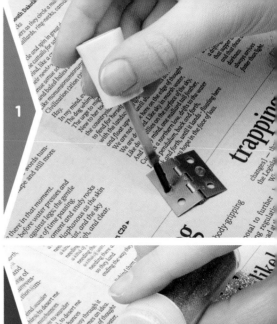

2. Sprinkle glitter on top of the nail polish. Let the nail polish dry completely.

3. Cut two pieces of ribbon 10 inches (25 cm) long.

4. Lay the hinges in a row. Thread one ribbon through the left holes of each hinge. Thread the second ribbon through the right holes.

5. Tie the ribbons around your wrist.

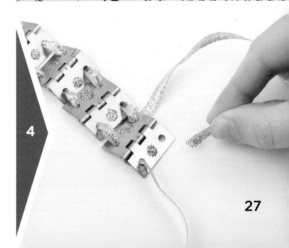

HARDWARE
HANDBag

A Tough & Charming Bag!

WHAT YOU NEED

NEWSPAPER

METAL HARDWARE
(HINGES, HEX NUTS,
BOLTS, WASHERS,
KEYS, BRACKETS)

GOLD SPRAY PAINT

FAUX LEATHER FOLDER

FABRIC GLUE

1. Cover your work surface with newspaper. Put the metal items on the newspaper. Paint the metal items. Follow the directions on the paint can. Let them dry at least 6 hours.

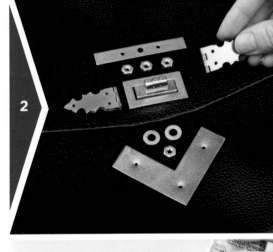

2. Arrange the metal items on the front of the folder.

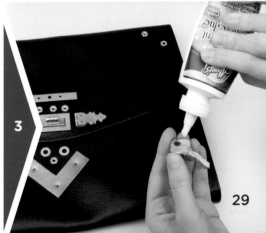

3. Glue the items in place. Let the glue dry.

Even Cooler!

Paint the folder before you glue the hardware for extra color!

CONCLUSION

Congratulations! You've just completed some fun projects using hardware. But don't stop here! Take what you've learned to the next step. Try out your own ideas for refashioning with hardware. Make something **unique** and totally you!

Check out the other books in this series. Learn how to refashion jeans, **scarves**, T-shirts, and more.

Get crafting today!

GLOSSARY

DESIGN – a decorative pattern or arrangement.

GARAGE – a room or building that cars are kept in.

OVERLAP – to make something lie partly on top of something else.

PERMISSION – when a person in charge says it's okay to do something.

SPRUCE UP – to make something look better.

STATEMENT – an opinion or attitude that you express through your appearance and actions.

STITCHING – a row or line of thread left in fabric by moving the needle in and out.

UNIQUE – different, unusual, or special.

WARDROBE – the clothes belonging to one person.

Websites

To learn more about Cool Refashion, visit **booklinks.abdopublishing.com**. These links are routinely monitored and updated to provide the most current information available.

INDEX